Surf
The Unofficia y

By Ryan August

BookCaps™ Study Guides
www.bookcaps.com

© 2012. All Rights Reserved.

Bell end Rider

Table of Contents

ABOUT LIFECAPS 3

INTRODUCTION 4

MORIARITY'S FIRST YEARS 5

A BRIEF GUIDE TO WAVES..7

    WHERE WAVES COME FROM 7
    THE PARTS OF A WAVE 8
    WAVE HEIGHT 9

MAVERICKS...11

    THE EARLY YEARS OF MAVERICKS......................................12
    TRAGEDY AT MAVERICKS 17
    COMPETITION AT MAVERICKS..20
    TRAINING FOR MAVERICKS 24

MORIARITY'S FIRST RIDE AT MAVERICK'S 31

    THE IRON CROSS AND THE COVER OF SURFER MAGAZINE....32

MORIARITY'S CAREER 37

MORIARITY'S DEATH 45

CHASING MAVERICKS 48

CONCLUSION..52

About LifeCaps

LifeCaps is an imprint of BookCaps™ Study Guides. With each book, a lesser known or sometimes forgotten life is is recapped. We publish a wide array of topics (from baseball and music to literature and philosophy), so check our growing catalogue regularly (**www.bookcaps.com**) to see our newest books.

Introduction

Jay Moriarity was a big wave surfer whose positive spirit, relentless dedication, and respect for his sport earned him the admiration of the entire surfing world. Although, he lost his life just one day before his 23rd birthday, he is still an inspiration to not just the surfing community, but to countless people that he met in his life.

Moriarity made his mark as a big wave surfer at Maverick's, a surf spot north of Half Moon Bay that is known for unforgiving waves that routinely top out above 30 feet high, rivaling those that are found on the North Shore of Oahu in Hawaii. After making his first ride at Maverick's at the age of 15, Moriarity went on to travel the world as a big wave "soul surfer" until his death in 2001.

Moriarity's First Years

James Michael Moriarity was born in Augusta, Georgia on June 16, 1978 to Christy and Doug Moriarity. His father, a former skydiver for the Green Berets, introduced him to surfing when he was just 11 years old. The family had relocated to the surfing mecca of Santa Cruz in Northern California, which has an ongoing rivalry with Huntington Beach in Southern California regarding which town is the true "Surf City." The two cities have even had legal battles over the right to own the "Surf City" label, which currently belongs to Huntington Beach.

Moriarity learned to surf at the popular break called Sewer Peak. He recalled that he did not even have a wetsuit and simply surfed in t-shirts and shorts on a three-inch thick board straight out of the 1970s, but it did not matter to him. He was hooked from the beginning. When his parents divorced, and his father was no longer a consistent figure in his life, surfing and spending time in the water was a way for Moriarity to deal with the pain.

It did not take long for Moriarity to find his true calling. At 12 years old, he won his first event. Competing in waves twice his size, in a National Scholastic Surfing Association (NSSA) shortboard contest, Moriarity realized that he was much more interested in surfing mountainous waves than in competition. Big wave surfing is a specialty and requires as much courage as skill. For a 12 year-old to want to participate in surfing, on this level, is unusual. It was even more rare for an adolescent to have to the ability to do it, but Moriarity showed he was not the typical teenage boy.

A Brief Guide to Waves

Understanding the enormity of Moriarity's achievement at successfully surfing at Maverick's, let alone doing it for the first time at 15 years of age, requires a base understanding of waves and how surfers view them. The image of a surfer as a beach bum is largely a myth. Regular surfers are students of the ocean and spend a terrific deal of time assessing weather conditions, and how they impact the ocean's waves. In many ways, surfers are similar to scientists and the ocean is their laboratory.

Where Waves Come From

Waves require wind and water. Waves can form in ponds, lakes, oceans, or even in a backyard swimming pool if there is enough wind. However, in order to surf a wave, the wave has to break. Waves do not break in deep water because the angle of the wave is not steep enough. Waves break in shallow water, closer to the shore, when they collide with a barrier, such as a reef.

Waves form swells as they organize and move in toward the shore. Some of the biggest waves are created by groundswells that travel thousands of miles over the water. Surfers often discuss swells because the size of the swells is an indicator of the size of the waves. A swell can last for hours, days, or, if surfers get lucky, weeks. When swells come in at a surf point, surfers will often say that it is "going off." A group of waves is called a set and the period of calm between sets is a lull, which is crucial for surfers to recognize when picking the right moment to paddle their boards out and ride the waves.

The Parts of a Wave

A surfer looks at a wave and sees more than beauty and size. Surfers analyze the different parts of a wave and talk about waves using the following terms.

Face: The wave's front. This is the part of the wave that a surfer rides.
Wall: The unbroken part of the wave's face that literally looks like a wall of water.
Shoulder: The unbroken part of a wave, near the top.
Peak: The wave's highest point, where it breaks.
Trough: The wave's bottom.
Lip: The tip of a cresting wave that rolls down.

Curl: It is remarkably similar to the wave's lip. It is the breaking part of the wave that curls toward the bottom of the wave.

Whitewater: When surfers talk about "the soup," they are referring to the frothy white water at the bottom of a broken wave.

Wave Height

Beginners often surf waves that are chest high, but big wave surfers can surf waves 50 feet tall or more. Falling, or wiping out, on a wave this powerful can drop a surfer 50 or 60 feet below the water's surface. This does not give a surfer much time to resurface and get out of the way before the next wave comes.

When surfers talk to each other about the size of a wave, they do not usually speak about height and inches. They use a typical body length as the primary descriptor.

Shoulder-high: A wave that reaches the shoulder.

Head-high: A wave as tall as a typical surfer.

Overheard: A wave that is taller than a typical surfer.

Double-overhead: A wave that is twice the size of a typical surfer.

Triple-overhead: A wave that is three times the size of a typical surfer.

Big wave surfers will not be interested in anything less than a double-overhead. A triple-overhead is preferred, which is enormous to the casual surfer, but even that pales in comparison to what Maverick's can offer.

Mavericks

Waves bigger than 12 feet are rare, which likely adds to the allure of finding them for big wave surfers. Just about 80 percent of all waves in the world are shorter than 12 feet and just under half are smaller than four feet tall. For the biggest waves – 35 feet or more – to develop, there needs to be a stretch of unobstructed ocean of anywhere between six and nine miles. Once those waves do develop and roll in toward a reef or some other barrier that creates a surf spot, they are monsters of wind-fueled energy capable of moving 30 to 60 knots per hour. These waves can create an incredible 6,000 pounds of pressure per square feet when they finally break. Daniel Duane wrote in "Caught Inside: A Surfer's Year on the California Coast," that surfing is the only way that man has figured out how to ride energy and will remain the only way "until someone figures out how to ride sound or light."

To surf any wave at all requires some combination of skill, coordination, and strength. Watching and analyzing a wave is just as valuable, if not more so, than the physical demands of paddling, popping up, turning, and even mastering the art of the wipeout. To catch a wave requires that a surfer move the surfboard at the same speed as the approaching swell. A 15-foot wave moves at approximately 20 miles per hour. In order to surf the enormous waves of 50 feet or more, surfers need to be towed in on a jet ski, as it is the only way to generate the necessary speed. There is some controversy in the surfing world about whether or not using machines to catch a wave detracts from the experience and if this can truly be called surfing. However, the biggest waves cannot be surfed without this type of assistance.

The Early Years of Mavericks

In 1958 or perhaps 1961, Alex Matienzo, Jim Thompson, and Dick Notmeyer "discovered" Maverick's at Pillar Point in Northern California and were, like most people, in awe of what they saw. The German Shepherd they brought with them seemed to have the most fun, but even the dog, Maverick, had to be leashed to the bumper of a car for fear he would be swept away by the ferocious surf. The dog did leave one legacy to the legendary surf point – his name. The surfers decided that he had the most fun there, so he should get to lend his name to the break and for many years, it was known as Maverick's Point. As for the surfers, the waves seemed out of reach for mere mortals.

It is with this information that Jeff Clark assessed the waves at Maverick's Point as a 17 year-old. He could see the waves breaking from the hills behind his high school at Half Moon Bay. Clark eventually went for a closer look and spent hours watching the waves through the fog. These were not the waves of the 1960s surf movies, with sunbathing teenagers frolicking in the warm water. The air at Maverick's is cool, and the water is even colder. Factor in the wind and the 25 – 30 foot waves and Clark's friends thought he was crazy to try surfing there. A friend was nearby the first time. The friend wanted no part of Maverick's Point, but watched to see if Clark was going to make it out alive and was prepared to call the Coast Guard if need be. Clark did make it out alive, and for the next 15 years after that, he surfed Maverick's alone, something that nobody would dare try to do today.

Maverick's quite simply scares most surfers. In 1992, when Ben Marcus, a writer for *Surfer* magazine went to Maverick's to see what all of the fuss was about, he wrote that it is "gloomy, isolated, inherently evil." Finding it is part of the battle for some surfers. It is located off the coast of Pillar Point, south of Ocean Beach in San Francisco and an hour north of Santa Cruz. It is easy to miss without knowing exactly where it is. Actually accessing the water is also challenging and requires navigating through the village of Princeton-by-the-Sea in Half Moon Bay, which has taken advantage of its legendary surf spot by naming everything from inns to locally brewed beer after Maverick's.

There is no beach at Maverick's, just an assortment of rocks. The water is frigid, nearly 30 degrees colder than the water off the coast of Hawaii. Maverick's is a reef break, which surfers typically like because they create the most consistent waves. Also, since the transition between deep to shallow water is so abrupt, reef breaks create some of the best barrel waves. The barrel wave is the iconic surfing wave in which a surfer appears to be literally enclosed in a long tube of water. At Maverick's, the drop-off beyond the reef is a steep 60 feet, which is a deep, chilly fall into the water for surfers who get thrown off of a wave. Wetsuits, which are a necessity, help surfers maintain some body heat, but their buoyancy also makes ducking under waves more challenging.

Waves at Maverick's can easily reach 25 feet and, in the midst of a particularly ferocious storm, they can top out over 80 feet high. Author Jon Krakauer wrote, "The difference between riding a head-high wave–the upper limit for most surfers–and riding a hollow, dredging 40-footer is the difference between driving 35 mph and driving 200 mph." What also makes Maverick's so frightening, as well as potentially deadly, are the hold-downs. When a surfer is dumped into the water, a wave may hold him or her underneath the water's surface, preventing the surfer from coming up for air. Most surfers have no difficulty holding their breath long enough to wait out one wave, but when a second giant wave crashes down on top of a surfer, the situation becomes more dangerous. Two-wave hold-downs are extremely common at Maverick's, and three-wave hold-downs are not unheard of.

Adding to the challenge of Maverick's is the potential for sharks. The water that surrounds the break is a seal habitat, which attracts great whites, although surfer Grant Washburn downplays their threat. "Sharks? Oh, they're around, but that's not even a concern out there. Way too many other things to worry about. You've got a half-dozen nightmare possibilities before you even get around to the sharks."

One of those possibilities is the potential of being hurtled toward a jagged area of rocks and boulders along the inner reef, fittingly called the Boneyard. Not only does a surfer risk broken bones and a ripped wet suit if tossed into the Boneyard, the waves relentlessly pin unlucky surfers in place until they can get up onto a rock or find an area to wait for rescue from a jet ski.

Even with all of this potential for disaster, Jeff Clark became a Maverick's regular and, between 1975 and 1990, he was the *only* regular. A winter swell on January 22, 1990 changed that. As the locals will do, Clark left his construction job and headed directly to Ocean Beach when he heard the surf forecast that day. By the time he got there, the waves were too choppy, and surfing was not possible, but Clark suspected that the swells were producing perfect barrel waves at Maverick's. He managed to talk two surfing buddies, Tom Powers and Dave Schmidt, into following him. When they arrived, they were astonished at the sight of the beautiful, barrel waves. Everyone managed to ride a couple that day and Maverick's was no longer Jeff Clark's personal haven.

Dave Schmidt's brother, Richard, was a renowned big-wave surfer who was in Hawaii as Maverick's was going off that day. Dave called his brother to tell him about his discovery, saying that the waves were large enough to drive semi-trucks through them. Richard found it difficult to believe that he would need, as his brother told him, his "big gun" to surf out at Pillar Point. In surfing lingo, a gun is a board and a whopping board, usually over nine feet long, is needed to surf mighty towering waves. It seemed impossible that such a place had been in his own backyard all of these years. However, when Richard surfed Maverick's and gave it his seal of approval, it was anointed as a legitimate giant wave surf point.

Clark and a small crew of surfers were still primarily the only ones that took on Maverick's for a while. Clark welcomed anyone prepared to try it, and anyone prepared for the worst case scenario. He was open with what he knew and relished the connection he had developed with the water. He said, "You feel your place in the universe when you're out there on the wave, that you are a small part of something much bigger." It is the preparation for the worst-case scenario that would one day save Jay Moriarity's life.

Tragedy at Mavericks

By 1994, Maverick's had firmly cemented its place as a big wave mecca, attracting big wave riders from around the world. In late December, Maverick's was going off and even in the days before Christmas, it was attracting a crowd of surfers, boats filled with photographers, and helicopters. For a week, Maverick's had been offering up some of biggest, perfectly formed waves that had been seen in years. The surfing community is a small one, and when three of the most highly regarded big wave surfers heard about what was happening at Maverick's, they hopped on a plane from Hawaii to get to the Bay Area.

Ken Bradshaw, Brock Little, and Mark Foo arrived in Northern California on December 23. Of the three, Foo was the best-known, due in part to his own promotion of himself as a living legend. The host of a cable television surfing show with the phone numbers of the best surfing photographers close at hand, Foo was not shy about his goal of surfing the biggest waves in the world, while making sure it was documented on film. He was known as a bit of a risk-taker, sometimes treating a gigantic wave like the smaller waves and being more aggressive than other surfers. Foo said, "If you want to ride the ultimate wave, you have to be willing to pay the ultimate price." He was one of the few surfers at the time that showed it was possible to make a living surfing the towering waves, even if there were few competitions available. He made his living by getting his accomplishments in print, on television, or wherever else he could and by racking up sponsorships.

Foo is both credited and blamed for showing that a decent wipeout photo could pay off. Nobody used to ever want to wipe out. Mark Renneker, a friend of Moriarity, said that he could not believe what he was seeing on the day that Foo arrived at Maverick's. He was disgusted that the best big wave surfers in the world were taking risks and making mistakes just because the cameras were there and they might get a sponsorship out of dramatic photo. Renneker said that Foo was making the same mistakes as everyone else, but Bradshaw disagreed about the only wave that Foo would ride at Maverick's that day. He said he was "right where he needed to be.

At first, Maverick's was not living up to its billing. Bradshaw called it "anti-climatic" and most of the surfers that were there were just hanging out and having fun until around noon when a extensive set rolled in. Bradshaw let the first set go by, then turned his board and paddled hard toward the next incoming set. He saw that Foo was ahead of him and charging to catch the same wave. Surfing etiquette says that Bradshaw had first claim to the wave because he was closer to the peak. In some scenarios, surfers have been known to get into fistfights in the ocean over territorial rights to waves. However, even though the wave should have been his, he backed off and let Foo have it and stopped paddling.

Surfers will pull up and throw their legs to either side of the board to stop their momentum, which is the equivalent of braking a car or a bike. As Bradshaw pulled up, the wave grew and knocked him off his board. As he was momentarily held in mid-air, he saw Foo moving toward the wave, about to pop up on his own board. Bradshaw did not see Foo get sucked over the falls of the giant wave – although nothing bigger than he had surfed before – and slam into the water before getting buried by a wall of water. His board shattered into three pieces. Nobody noticed, though, that Foo never resurfaced. About an hour later, Evan Slater saw a black blob that some initially insisted was just kelp. Slater dove into the water and pulled Foo's dead body into a boat. With dozens of surfers and photographers on hand, nobody noticed that Mark Foo had drowned. Maverick's had claimed its first victim.

Competition at Mavericks

Four years later in 1998, after Jay Moriarity's first ride and Foo's death, Clark announced that there would be a giant wave contest at Maverick's. Suddenly, attention was back on Maverick's after Foo's death had quieted some of the frenzy. Called "Men Who Ride Mountains," Clark said that the competition would be open only to surfers who regularly rode the waves at Maverick's because he did not want anyone out there who did not understand what they were getting into. That meant that some of the biggest names in professional surfing were not invited, although Clark said that most of the pro surfers were too scared to try Maverick's, anyway.

The Maverick's Invitational chooses 24 surfers, along with a group of alternates, who get 24 hours notice that the competition will begin. The waves dictate when the contest is held, so if the waves do not cooperate, there is no contest. The first big wave competition at Maverick's was won by Darryl "Flea" Virostko. He won again in 2000 and then the contest was not held again until 2004. Flea won that year, too, technically giving him a three-peat. What a lot of his fellow surfers did not know is that Flea, known as a fearless rider, was battling an addiction to methamphetamine, perhaps fueling his fearless attitude. When he reached his 40s, Flea retired from surfing Maverick's, drug-free but with some regret at not taking better care of his body when he was younger.

Issues with sponsorships, poor weather, and hard feelings have plagued the competition at Maverick's. Clark had worked out a deal with Quiksilver to sponsor the event in 1999 and 2000, but in 2001, Quiksilver did not want to call the contest, even though it looked like the perfect swell was heading toward Pillar Point. The company also sponsored the big-wave contest at Waimea Bay in honor of Hawaiian surfer Eddie Aikau who was lost at sea in 1978. "The Eddie" had just been completed, and Quiksilver wanted at least five or six weeks between contests. In fact, the Maverick's Big Wave Invitational, as it is now called, was not held six out of the first 13 years of the event. In 2011, it was renamed for Moriarity and given the nickname, "The Jay," but The Jay Moriarity Foundation requested that his name not be associated with the event during all of the turmoil. Clark ended up suing Maverick Surf Ventures, the company he founded. He eventually returned as contest director in 2011. In 2012, the contest joined the Big Wave World Tour, which includes stops in Chile, Mexico, and Peru.

Mark Foo is not the only surfer that lost his life at Maverick's. In January 2011, there was a close call when a massive wave caused several surfers to wipe out, including Jacob Trette, who was also sucked over the falls and nearly drowned after being pummeled on the rocks. He was found unconscious and floating in the water by a photographer who was riding a jet ski. Ironically, personal water craft are illegal in the area, but it saved Trette's life on this day.

Two months later, 35 year-old welder and surfer from Hawaii, Sion Milosky, was nearing the end of a hugely successful day at Maverick's but would not be as fortunate as Trette. It was close to 6 p.m. and Milosky had impressed his fellow surfers with his rides on waves that reached as high as 45 feet. For most of the surfers, the waves were simply too hot to handle, but Milosky was known as a surfer who would ride just about anything. In 2010, he was named the "Underground Surfer of the Year," as part of a group of surfers that does not care about photographs or other publicity, but simply surfs to surf.

As Milosky took off for an especially nasty wave, the other surfers watched from the channel, hooting and yelling encouragement. He rode the wave to the bottom and made a turn, but he ran into a huge wall of water when the lip of the wave he was riding collapsed. Milosky was plunged into the water and forced down by a two-wave hold-down. Everyone waited for Milosky to resurface, but when he didn't, another surfer hopped on a jet ski and went to find him. His body was discovered about 20 minutes later, but he could not be revived. There were no obvious signs of damage to his body, leaving Jeff Clark to simply look at the water days later and "reflect on the ocean and what it can do."

Maverick's regulars have had an ongoing battle with the National Oceanic and Atmospheric Association (NOAA) and the Monterey Bay National Marine Sanctuary. Because of the surf point's location, personal water craft are banned in an effort to protect the nearby wildlife. The banned area covers 275 miles of California coast that stretches from Cambria to Marin County. However, many of the surfers are upset at what they view as the priority off marine life over human life, and the ban is regularly violated. Often, it is photographers who man the jet skis. The day that Milosky died, more surfers were wiping out than completing a successful ride. Clark said two days before Milosky's death that he personally had pulled 10 surfers out of the water using a jet ski. He said, "If NOAA and the National Marine Sanctuary put no value on human life, it's a law that needs to be broken."

Training for Mavericks

Surfers relish so-called overhead days and Moriarity had his share of them at Pleasure Point, where he was a regular. Pleasure Point has long been a surfing mecca in Santa Cruz, although its name comes from the speakeasies that sprung up during Prohibition, not because of the epic waves. Still, when there were overhead days at Pleasure Point, Moriarity was out there. Like many big wave surfers, though, he had a desire for something more. In 1991, when Moriarity was 13, rumors about Maverick's had started to spread through the surfing community in Santa Cruz. Moriarity heard about it while eavesdropping on a conversation between Rick "Frosty" Hesson and another surfer. It sounded like a dream come true to Moriarity. This is what he wanted to do, but to find out more about Maverick's, he had to summon up the guts to approach Hesson.

Frosty Hesson was 45 years old when the teenage Moriarity began to get the idea that he wanted to surf Mavericks. A gruff and intimidating construction worker, he was also already a legendary surfing coach. He was teaching construction classes at San Jose State University, coaching surfing at Soquel High School, and taking individual surfers under his wing when he met Moriarity. He was skeptical when Moriarity approached him, but, at the same time, he was impressed that Moriarity recognized that he was not going to learn to surf Maverick's by hanging out with other adolescent boys. Hesson agreed to teach Moriarity but only on the condition that he brought him a signed permission slip from his mother. Moriarity complied, and with that, he began a two-year training session to prepare him for Maverick's.

With ten years of coaching to his credit, Hesson had developed his own unique style of attacking waves. For Moriarity, there was much work to do before he would ever see Maverick's. Hesson's first order of business was to see if Moriarity was willing to put in the work, and he found Moriarity to be an eager student. Hesson wanted Moriarity to develop his ability to analyze and sharpen his critical thinking skills. Before surfing Maverick's, Moriarity had to become a student of surfing, and in Hesson's surf school, homework was required. One of the first tasks for Moriarity was to write a two-page essay. Hesson said, "Most people don't understand that the shortcut to improvement in your surfing is understanding and thinking. The best way to understand your thinking process about anything is to write it down."

Moriarity completed the essay the next day, and when he rushed back to Hesson's Chevy Astrovan to show his teacher what he had done, he found a note taped to the van's window. Hesson left him a list of 15 more essay topics. Moriarity recalled that each of the 55 essays that he ended up writing for Hesson had to be rewritten, not once, but three times. When he was done, Moriarity had written 330 pages. Each essay was followed by an in-depth classroom discussion, with the front seat of Hesson's van serving as the classroom. Moriarity and Hesson spent so much time in the van that Hesson went through six replacement dome lights. The topics often had, on the surface, very little to do with surfing. Hesson asked Moriarity to think about esoteric questions such as what he would do if he knew he was going to die tomorrow. Moriarity and Hesson were not always alone. Moriarity's girlfriend, Kim, was often in the back of the van, listening to the philosophical discussions. Kim and Jay were married after they eloped and went to Lake Tahoe, Nevada in 2000.

Hesson also coached Moriarity on the art of visualization. Moriarity imagined himself on the waves and taking note of the simplest details such as the angle of the sun, the speed of the wave, and the velocity of the wind. Hesson walked Moriarity through countless "virtual" surfing sessions at Maverick's, always visualizing positive outcomes but putting him in scenarios where he had to do the right things to avoid a negative outcome. Hesson's goal for Moriarity was to help him avoid panicking when something went wrong. He believes that panic sets in when there is nothing to back up "Plan A" when "Plan A" fails. Not only did Moriarity have Plans B, C, and D, Hesson said, "Jay has been to Plan E."

Moriarity possessed an internal drive to both learn and compete. Hesson never forced Moriarity to do anything, but he over time, he realized Moriarity was listening. During a swim session with some other surfers, Hesson had to go to the aide of one of his swimmers who somehow lost his swim trunks. When Hesson made it back toward the front of the pack, he saw that Moriarity was a full body length ahead of surfing legend, Robert "Wingnut" Weaver. Hesson was impressed, but did not tell Moriarity that, saying, "It's not my job to tell him that I'm impressed."

Other elements to Moriarity's Maverick's preparation included running, bike riding, and beach volleyball. In the beginning, Hesson did not work out with him, testing him to see if he would lose interest and quit. Moriarity did not quit, and after six months, Hesson joined him in his rides and swims. By the summer of 1992, Hesson was confident that Moriarity had trained his body and his mind enough to take on Maverick's. That winter, he told Moriarity he was ready, but surfing is subject to conditions and the conditions did not permit any surfing at Maverick's in the 1992-1993 season.

Hesson and Moriarity went to Maverick's anyway, and Moriarity's preparation continued. They went out during minus tide, or an unusually low tide, to assess the reef and draw diagrams. They paddled out to the water and did even more analysis of how Moriarity would handle the waves when the time finally came. Hesson was adamant that Moriarity know what to do when the two-wave hold-down came, which Hesson was certain would come. By this point, Hesson had been surfing Maverick's for six years and shared everything he could, much of which he was reluctant to make public information. Hesson's fear was that other surfers would think that simply reading what he had to say would be enough preparation to go out and surf Maverick's.

Moriarity also had the innate qualities of a waterman already in him by the time he started his training with Hesson. Any surfer has an appreciation of the ocean and Moriarity's final stages of training into the summer of 1993 found him in the water regularly. Moriarity not only surfed, but he sailed, he fished, and he paddled, once covering 35 miles across Monterey Bay. It was all part of his training and gaining a deeper understanding of and a respect for the water that is essential to successfully surfing Maverick's.

Moriarity's First Ride at Maverick's

By the time Moriarity paddled out to catch his first wave at Maverick's, he and Hesson had moved beyond student/teacher to friends and comrades in their love of the water. Like Hesson, Moriarity would be woken from his sleep in the middle of the night, sensing that Maverick's was going off. However, even though Moriarity was ready, it was not a sure thing that Maverick's was ready for him in the surfing season of 1993 – 1994. Like the previous season, the swells were small.

Finally, it was time on April 1, 1994. Hesson had a broken rib and only paddled out part of the way. In surfing, surfers paddle out on their boards and wait their turn in the lineup, similar to a bullpen in baseball. When Moriarity realized that Hesson was not near him anymore and was going to watch from the channel, he momentarily wondered if he should wait or if he should go take his place in the lineup with the Maverick's regulars. Then, it occurred to him that only he would know if he was ready to grab a wave, so he kept paddling out and joined the lineup. The first wave that 15 year-old Moriarity rode at Maverick's was between 15 and 18 feet high, and when it was over, both Moriarity and Hesson were ecstatic. Moriarity said he felt like he had climbed Mount Everest or won a gold medal at the Olympics. Hesson said watching Moriarity's joy was like watching "a kid in a candy store." Moriarity's training was over, but the lessons that Hesson taught him would prove to be critical during the next surfing season.

The Iron Cross and the Cover of Surfer Magazine

The night of December 18, 1994, Moriarity was working a shift at Pleasure Point Pizza. After several phone calls to the National Weather Service, he realized that the waves he had been anticipating for the next day were going to be even bigger than he realized. When his shift was over, he went out for a night surfing session at Pleasure Point to think about what tomorrow would hold for him.

At 5 a.m. the next day, Moriarity loaded his mother's pickup with two ten-foot surfboards and took off for Maverick's. When he arrived an hour later, he knew the waves were going to be big, probably bigger than he had ever seen. He was right. The waves that day were bigger than anything surfers had faced to date, other than in Hawaii. Photographers and other surfers had started to arrive when Moriarity hitched a ride on a boat rented by photographer Bob Barbour. The air temperature was in the 40s, and a steady wind out of the northeast made it seem even colder.

At 7 a.m., ten surfers had already braved the frigid water. Moriarity watched and thought the waves looked "huge and perfect," but he also considered that there might be too much wind. Some wind is favourable, but too much wind makes it impossible to hear and blows spray off the front of the board back into a surfer's face, making the takeoff challenging. As he watched, Moriarity reminded himself to stay low to get through the wind.

Moriarity was watching when Evan Slater got up on his board with no problem, but then the wind came up and brushed him off like a gnat. Slater, who was also surfing Maverick's for the first time that day, fell midway down the face of the wave, bounced twice, then disappeared as the water thrashed his body around. Surfers yelled and watched anxiously until Slater's head popped up above the whitewater, 100 feet from where he went down. Unphased, Moriarity zipped up his wetsuit, complete with two pairs of booties and two pairs of gloves. The water temperature was 52 degrees when he slipped over the side of the boat.

Moriarity picked his first wave of the day and went directly to the peak and got on his feet. He had told himself to say low to penetrate the wind, but the wind was too strong to permit that. He got caught in the lip of the wave, momentarily suspended in the air, and then made a 30 or 40 foot free-fall directly to the ocean floor. The wave exploded, and Moriarity disappeared. Flea Virostko looked over his shoulder and saw Moriarity in his free-fall and thought there was no way he could survive. It never occurred to Moriarity that he would die, though. He had been trained too well to panic, but that did not mean that the surfers and photographers watching did not have anxious moments when Moriarity did not appear after 12, then 20 seconds. It was not just when he surfaced after the two-wave hold-down, completely unharmed from one of the most brutal wipeouts ever seen that he earned the respect of the regulars at Maverick's. It was when he went out again. And again. And again. Moriarity was doing what he loved best and, as always, he did it with a smile on his face.

He stayed in the icy water for five more hours and caught eight waves after that wipeout. What he did not know is that Bob Barbour had his camera trained on him the entire time he rode his first wave. Barbour had captured Moriarity in midflight, his board directly in front of him. The only parts of his body that can be seen in the photo are his arms, outstretched so that his body and board form a cross against the green wave. The shot, now known as the "Iron Cross," made the May 1995 issue of *Surfer*, the same edition that chronicled Mark Foo's death later that week. The cover shot is a photo of Moriarity, just as he was about to drop into the 30-foot wave. Suddenly, 16 year-old Moriarity was one of the most famous big wave surfers in the world. Barbour said that he was watching Moriarity because he knew he was out there with a mission to prove himself that day. "The waves were big, and he was going for it.... When you look at him there, at the top of the wave, you see so much grace." Moriarity did not like the Iron Cross shot, though. To him, it was a photo of an error, and he was not happy with himself that he took off so late in a crosswind and put himself in such a dangerous situation.

After his epic day of surfing, Moriarity called his mentor and recounted what had happened out at Maverick's. Hesson had heard through the grapevine, already, and silently listed as Moriarity told him that after the horrific wipeout, he went back to the boat to get the backup board that Hesson had loaned him so that he could keep surfing. Finally, Moriarity told Hesson the real reason he had called. "What you taught me saved my life. If you hadn't helped me train and practice all those things, I would have died. And I just wanted to thank you."

Moriarity's Career

Moriarity did not surf because he wanted to win tournaments and lure a slew of corporate sponsors. This was made clear when he was an adolescent and committed his body and mind to training for Maverick's. Very few big wave surfers can do it full time, especially since the season is limited. Moriarity was going to be a firefighter, having just passed his EMT exam at Cabrillo College when he died.

Like most big wave surfers, Moriarity did not pursue it because it offers exciting career opportunities. It doesn't. Nearly 10 years after Moriarity's death, Evan Slater said that he could count on one hand the number of surfers that make a living at it. This is despite the fact that big wave surfing has gained more of a foothold in the surfing – and sporting – world. Documentaries such as "Step into Liquid" and "Riding Giants" have captured the imagination of land-lovers as they get an up-close view of big wave surfers riding waves that most people run from. The Billabong XXL Awards, which offer large cash prizes to the best big wave riders of the year, had its 12-year anniversary in 2012 and is broadcast on national television. Even the Maverick's Invitational has a webcast. The world of big wave surfing has come a long way from when Moriarity first paddled out to Maverick's as a 15 year-old, but it is still primarily pursued for the satisfaction of it, whatever that means to each surfer.

Moriarity did compete. He was asked to participate in the first two "Men Who Ride Mountains" invitationals at Maverick's in 1999 and 2000. Hesson competed in the 1999 event, too, at 50 years old. Moriarity did not win either competition, although there were several surfers who claimed that he should have at least had the chance to advance to the finals in the 2000 event. Some suggested out loud at the afterparty that he outsurfed the legendary Kelly Slater in an epic semi-final, at times riding behind him on the same wave. However, it was Slater, not Moriarity, who advanced on to the final. True to form, Moriarity said nothing about it, as it was not his style to complain. Ironically, Slater, who finished second and is the most decorated surfer in the world, did not return to surf at Maverick's for many years after that experience. He admitted that it scared him a bit, and it was not until 2010 that he said he wanted to compete again, although contest organizers thought it was a joke when they first heard the news.

Moriarity picked up a big-name sponsor, too. He signed with O'Neill, the iconic company that was started by fellow Santa Cruz resident and surfing legend Jack O'Neill. O'Neill is credited with inventing the wetsuit and making it possible for surfers to attack the waves in cool waters. Moriarity also traveled the world, often taking his wife with him to some of the best surfing spots on the planet. Not forgetting his roots, he was known to buy toys and souvenirs and take them home to give to children in the Pleasure Point community.

In 1997, Moriarity, Wingnut Weaver, and Richard Schmidt served as instructors in the inaugural year of the O'Neill Surf Academy. The purpose of the academy is to introduce children in Europe to surfing, and by the fourth year, Moriarity was picked to be the lead instructor. He had planned to meet Kim in Europe for the O'Neill tour in 2001, but, unfortunately, he did not live to see the academy's fourth season. Moriarity also coauthored a book with Chris Gallagher, a professional surfer turned coach. The two surfers wrote "The Ultimate Guide to Surfing," published in June 2001.

However, none of these things explain why Moriarity surfed or the type of surfer he was. Moriarity was a modern day soul surfer. It is a term that developed in the 1960s and, loosely defined, it implies someone who surfs simply for the pleasure of it. There is more to it than that for someone like Moriarity, though. He said of surfing, "It's an art, by the way you can express yourself on a wave. It's a sport, because you can compete with it, and it's spiritual because it's just you and Mother Nature. For me, it's very spiritual."

Spirituality is an essential element of surfing for the soul surfer. Scholar and conservationist Bron Taylor claims that for soul surfers, it is a "religious form in which a specific sensual practice constitutes its sacred center and the corresponding experiences are constructed in a way that leads to a belief in nature as powerful, transformative, healing, and sacred." And so it was for Moriarity. He surfed, in part, for the connection to nature. In the book Moriarity wrote with Gallagher, soul surfing is described as a "powerful, elemental activity" that is done "for the pure act of riding on a pulse of nature's energy, and the contentment this instills in the heart."

Big wave surfers like Moriarity take the spirituality of surfing to a different level with the sheer danger of what they attempt. Greg Noll is considered the father of big wave surfing. In 1957, as a 20 year-old living in Hawaii, he watched the waves at Waimea Bay on the North Shore. Now, it is known as one of the prime big wave surfing locations in the world. In 1957, nobody had ever dared to try such a thing. Noll said, "People really believed that if you paddled out at Waimea, there was going to be this vortex, and there would go all the *haoles* (Hawaiian for white person) flushed down the toilet." Even Hawaiians thought surfing those waves were impossible until Noll did it in. Then, in the winter of 1969, as many were evacuating due to the convergence of three enormous storms over the Pacific Ocean, Noll sat on Mahaka Beach, contemplating what he was seeing. For two hours, he watched Mother Ocean build up walls of water four to five stories high, only to detonate them seconds later. Then he went for it, paddled out, and rode a 35-foot tall wave, the biggest wave ever ridden up to that time.

Why do big wave surfers do it? The risks are far greater than shortboard surfing, which could explain why shortboarding is much more common. Falling off a wave shoots surfers underwater at an alarming speed. The change in air pressure can break lung capillaries and puncture ear drums. Breaking bones from being plunged to the ocean floor or tossed like a rag doll off of rocks or pieces of broken surf boards are as common as pulled muscles in a health club. As much as Moriarity loved surfing, it is crucial to note that he was also a skydiver, the epitome of risktaking as a hobby. Certainly there is a direct line connection between the feeling of riding on top of a 30-foot wave and dropping out of the sky. Moriarity said, "A good dose of fear is soothing for the human psyche. When the brain detects danger, the human body sends out norepinephrine to every part of the body. Once this danger has passed, the body sends out dopamine to the brain, a pleasurable chemical, as a way to congratulate the brain for surviving. These chemicals are what make people want to surf big waves."

Moriarity said waves were "the moving canvas," waiting for him to create art. Soul surfers view their surfing as a form of expression that is concert with the ocean, not a mastery of it. Soul surfers, like Moriarity, understand that they are never superior to Mother Ocean. They ride the waves to connect to the ocean, not defeat it. Moriarity's co-author said, "I think the soul comes into it more when a surfer appreciates nature and the true gift of surfing. Much of the satisfaction comes, not from a nice turn, but from the journey and the connection made with nature. Dolphins, whales, fish, birds, trees, sunsets – take these things away, and you strip a perfect wave of its soul."

One of Moriarity's best rides at Maverick's was one of his last. On January 19, 2001, it was more like a Southern California day than a day at Maverick's. The air was warm and the sun was shining. Well past sunset, Moriarity went out with Jeff Clark for a tow-in session. The godfather of Maverick's was so impressed with Moriarity that they had become towing partners. Clark was driving while the rest of the surfers watched, too exhausted from the day to do anything other than to see what Moriarity would do. He immediately went into what surfers call a square wave, or one in which the width of the tube is greater than the length. Moriarity rode in the tube for what seemed like an eternity to everyone who watched, who yelled as they watched ride the gigantic peeling wave. One of the surfers said that everyone was "screaming for 10 minutes," while his friend Mike Gerhardt said he was too terrified for Moriarity to scream. "It looked like death," he said. After the ride was over, Clark picked him up, and Moriarity did it again, now at least an hour after sunset. Later, at dinner when everyone talked about what they had just witnessed, Gerhardt said, "it was an incredible treat to witness the height of Jay's career, than night, right then and there."

Moriarity's Death

It is not uncommon for big wave surfers to free dive. It is simply diving into the depth of the ocean without the aid of a breathing apparatus. For surfers who ride the monster waves, the ability to hold their breath during a two-wave hold-down is the difference between life and death. Free diving is sound practice. Moriarity was asked to do a photo shoot for O'Neill at the Lohifushi resort in the Maldives in the Indian Ocean. The day before his 23rd birthday, he went out with a group of Brazilians to free dive and practice holding his breath for Mavericks.

Free drivers will hold on to a buoy rope to help them find their way back to the water's surface, although on this day, Moriarity went further down the rope than anyone else. This was not a significant cause for concern. It was Jay Moriarity, and it was assumed that he knew what he was doing, and he was left to train alone. Unfortunately, nobody noticed when Moriarity did not resurface. It was only when he missed both lunch and dinner that a crew went out to look for him. The divers thought that there was a chance they would find him if he had simply hyperventilated and regained consciousness as he ascended back to the top.

However, he was found near the bottom of the rope. With so little body fat and likely with his lungs full of water, he was negatively buoyant and laying on the ocean floor. He was in the water for nine hours before anyone discovered that Moriarity had drowned. One of the rescue divers that found him said, "Jay's unlikely death, in the depths of the warm tropical waters of the Maldives, seemed as far away from the chilly waters of Mavericks as you could get. Yet somewhere in between that contradiction was the realization that no matter where you are, our great mother ocean can never be fully mastered, even by the most committed waterman".

While exactly what happened to Jay is unknown, Kim Moriarity believes that he had a shallow-water blackout before he was able to climb back up the rope to the top. A shallow-water blackout is similar to fainting in the water. In the years following his death, she has clarified the point several times that Jay was not being reckless, but was training to do what he loved and simply had a tragic accident. His friend, Mike Gerhardt did not view it that way and was upset that Moriarity died in this manner. He said he wished that the other divers had paid more attention, but more than anything, he wished that Moriarity had listened when others had told him not to free dive alone. Three years after Jay died, Kim went to the location of the accident, hoping to gain some understanding and healing for the grief that overwhelmed her, and replicated the dive.

Following Jay's death, Kim said she was "numb." "I was upside down, turned around in the dark. I was uncomfortable in my own skin. I didn't know what to do with myself. I was lost." It is a tradition when a surfer dies to have a memorial surface called a paddle out. Friends, family, and community members paddle out on surfboards to a location that is meaningful to the surfer who has died, often carrying flowers or wearing leis. They form a circle, hold hands, and pray. Sometimes, the surfer's ashes are scattered on the water. Even though she was there, Kim does not remember the paddle out in Santa Cruz to memorialize Jay. She was grateful for the community of Santa Cruz, though. Surfers can be territorial and engage in some vicious turf wars, but Kim recalled "the longboarders, the shortboarders, the land lovers, everyone just came together. Even people who were enemies, on that day, none of that mattered. Even they were holding each other's hands. Our love for Jay was what brought us all there."

Chasing Mavericks

Kim is highly protective of Jay's legacy. Movie producers who wanted to tell Jay's particularly compelling story approached her repeatedly, but she was not ready for that for many years. The grief was too intense, and she was worried that she was not in the right mental condition to ensure that his story was told correctly. A movie about Jay's life was finally filmed in 2011. The process of working with the producers of "Chasing Mavericks," which includes Academy Award winner Curtis Hanson, took a long time. Slowly, Kim shared stories, memories, photographs, and scrapbooks about her life with Jay. Over time, she developed trust that the movie producers have Jay's best interest at heart.

Hesson was also skeptical. He had heard movie pitches before. When producers Brandon Hooper and Jim Meenaghan approached him, he said, "What kind of story do you want to tell?" When they told Hesson that they wanted to tell the real story, Hesson asked what they thought the real story was. Hooper and Meenaghan said, "Well, you know what it is. That's why we're talking to you." That is when Hesson knew he could listen to what they had to say. Ironically, Meenaghan met Jay in the mid-1990s when he was at a surf shop looking for a wetsuit for his girlfriend. An employee noticed him staring at the "Iron Cross" shot of Moriarity on the wall and told him that the guy who was helping him pick out a wetsuit was the surfer in the photo. Ten years later, Hooper was also searching for a wetsuit and the person that helped him with his purchase was Kim Moriarity.

The film was originally set to star Sean Penn as Hesson, but ultimately Gerard Butler got the part. He got a harrowing taste of what Maverick's can do in December 2011. Butler was filming on location at Maverick's and was surfing with Greg Long, Peter Mel, and Zach Wormhoudt, who consulted on the film. A surfer caught in the front of a wave break is said to be "caught inside," which can be a frightening situation for any surfer. It is similar to being caught in a washing machine, which is where the actor found himself on a day that reminded many of the day that Jacob Trette nearly drowned.

As Butler and the other surfers sat on their boards on the inside, a large set of outside waves came in and surprised them, knocking them off their boards. The surfers knew how to handle the situation, but Butler was knocked under water for a two-wave hold-down, and then took four or five more waves on the head before a jet ski was able to rescue him. He spent a night in the hospital for observation but made a full recovery. After the incident, Butler said, "It was a pretty close call. These waves came out of nowhere. I was with three of the best surfers in the world, and they were shouting, 'Paddle, Gerry, paddle!'. But this wave spread across the skyline, 30 feet high, and just dived on us, and it took me. It ripped off my safety leash so there was nothing to pull me back up. I was just tumbling, tumbling, tumbling...going, going. I was thinking, 'I need to get up!'. Then I felt the next wave hit, and it all started again."

Casting for the part of Jay was more challenging. It was crucial to not only capture the essence of his spirit, but they needed to find someone who could surf. In an ironic twist, Jonny Weston, an accomplished surfer, read the movie's script on the day before his 23rd birthday. Weston got the part, and when Kim saw him, she was taken aback by his similarity to Jay, and she felt that somehow, he had a hand in picking Weston for the role. Even though Weston can surf, it took six stunt doubles to recreate Moriarity's feats at Mavericks. Big wave surfer Anthony Tashnick handled most of the duty.

The movie's producers said that they wanted to make the film as authentic as possible. They hired Bob Pearson, who created Moriarity's boards, to make 173 boards for the movie. The wet suits were from O'Neill, like Moriarity wore, and nearly every prominent big wave surfer in the Santa Cruz area was involved as a consultant or stunt double. However, the level of authenticity for the paddle out after Moriarity's death was eerie for Kim. "When I saw that outrigger out in the water, time really kind of slowed down for me. It was almost like I astrally left my body. I could feel the energy in the air. It wasn't a movie set. It was like the real deal all over again."

The recreation of that day in June 2001 allowed Kim to be fully present the second time around. She paddled out with the unpaid extras and cried when she saw the rows of people, many of whom knew Jay and were truly there to celebrate him, not just be part of a movie. She said, "This community nurtured Jay and helped turned him into what he became. It's a tribe. Everyone looks out for each other." She and Hesson took the time to go to a local park that was being used as a staging area to thank everyone for participating. Hesson said of the scene, "It's so funny that you can feel that much emotion in the air...it was just all love."

Conclusion

Jay Moriarity did not change surfing, but he did remind others why they surf. In a retrospective look at his life, ten years after his death in the Maldives, Carlos Burle, a Brazilian surfer and the first Big Wave World Champion in 2010, said that Moriarity was "the kid who brought us all back together." Like many sports, the surfing community is prone to fracturing. Longboarders and shortboarders can be critical of each other; there are geographic rivalries, and there can even be conflict on the same wave. Numerous surfers recall that while some view grabbing a wave as a competition akin to "high stakes poker," Moriarity was always willing to share, which made them want to share with him. Bob Pearson, recalled, "I've worked with hundreds of surfers. I know what their egos can be like. Jay was different. He was the best, but he treated everyone as his equals. There was always a friendly warmth in his eyes."

Perhaps this is rooted in Moriarity's view of surfing as a spiritual experience. He did not view a wave as something that belonged to him, but as something that was gifted to him by nature. Even with the conflict that can plague the surfing community, there is still a bond that unites them, as a whole. Pearson said that the bond is "built out of a respect for the ocean, and for the way each one takes on the challenges."

Kim Moriarity started The Jay Moriarity Foundation shortly after his death. It provides funding to many local charities that benefit the Santa Cruz community and the environment. She stepped away from The Foundation and from Santa Cruz for a while but eventually returned to both. The Foundation also hosts the Surftech Jay Race in Santa Cruz, which brings in paddlers from around the country in prone and stand-up paddleboard racing, as well as swimming events. Nicknamed "The Jay Race," its mission to encourage paddlers, regardless of age or gender, to come together in friendly competition and to celebrate Moriarity's memory. Proceeds go to local junior lifeguard organizations.

"Live Like Jay" has become a catchphrase throughout Santa Cruz and stickers with the slogan can be seen just about anywhere that surfers congregate. Kim said that it is necessary for people to understand what the slogan does and does not mean. "It doesn't mean to live exactly like Jay did. You don't need to be a gnarly athlete and big wave rider. It means you should live to be who you truly are meant to be, and to be true to yourself."

Cover Image © homydesign - Fotolia.com

Printed in Great Britain
by Amazon.co.uk, Ltd.,
Marston Gate.